FINANCIAL FREEDOM

PROVEN STEPS TO ACCUMULATING WEALTH AND UNDERSTANDING PASSIVE MONEY

by **Kevin D. Peterson**

Descrierea CIP a Bibliotecii Naționale a României
KEVIN D. PETERSON
   Financial Freedom. Proven Steps To Accumulating Wealth And Understanding Passive Money, by Kevin D. Peterson. – Bucharest: My Ebook Publishing House, 2018
   ISBN 978-606-983-626-2

FINANCIAL FREEDOM
PROVEN STEPS TO ACCUMULATING WEALTH AND UNDERSTANDING PASSIVE MONEY

by **Kevin D. Peterson**

My Ebook Publishing House
Bucharest, 2018

CONTENTS

Chapter 1. AN INTRODUCTION TO FINANCIAL FREEDOM 11

Chapter 2. ACTIVE INCOME 16

Chapter 3. PASSIVE INCOME 21

Chapter 4. HOW TO ACHIEVE FINANCIAL FREEDOM 36

Chapter 5. WHAT SHOULD FINANCIAL FREEDOM MEAN TO ME? 51

Conclusion 54

INTRODUCTION

I want to use this means to thank and congratulate you for downloading this book **"Financial Freedom: Proven Steps To Accumulating Wealth And Understanding Passive Money"**

This book is a concise and interactive guide to understanding the concept of financial freedom, the two major types of income that relate to financial freedom and ways to achieve this most sought after freedom.

It also contains insight as to what financial freedom may mean to different categories of people and the traits that anyone who seeks financial freedom should imbibe.

Thanks for downloading this book. I hope you find this book an interesting read with impactful lessons to learn.

Copyright 2018 by Zen Mastery - All rights reserved

This document is geared towards providing exact and reliable information in regards to the topic and issue covered. The publication is sold with the idea that the publisher is not required to render accounting, officially permitted, or otherwise, qualified services. If advice is necessary, legal or professional, a practiced individual in the profession should be ordered.

- From a Declaration of Principles which was accepted and approved equally by a Committee of the American Bar Association and a Committee of Publishers and Associations.

In no way is it legal to reproduce, duplicate, or transmit any part of this document in either electronic means or in printed format. Recording of this publication is strictly prohibited and any storage of this document is not allowed unless with written permission from the publisher. All rights reserved.

The information provided herein is stated to be truthful and consistent, in that any liability, in terms of inattention or otherwise, by any usage or abuse of any policies, processes, or directions contained within is the solitary and utter responsibility of the recipient reader. Under no circumstances will any legal responsibility or blame be held against the publisher for any reparation, damages, or monetary loss due to the information herein, either directly or indirectly.

Respective authors own all copyrights not held by the publisher.

The information herein is offered for informational purposes solely, and is universal as so. The presentation of the information is without contract or any type of guarantee assurance.

The trademarks that are used are without any consent, and the publication of the trademark is without permission or backing by the trademark owner. All trademarks and brands within this book are for clarifying purposes only and are the owned by the owners themselves, not affiliated with this document.

CHAPTER 1

AN INTRODUCTION TO FINANCIAL FREEDOM

The sense of freedom is one sure feeling that everyone likes to have especially as regards finances. Nobody (or at least, no rational person) wants to be always dependent on another for livelihood for a long period.

So, this book will serve to help you learn about and be abreast with the concept of financial freedom or and it entails as well as a few tips on how to cash in the opportunities around you to be financially free, or in my own words, financially empowered.

What is Financial freedom?

This happens to be the big question here, doesn't it? Let's see how well it can be answered.

Freedom is the sense of being able to do whatever one wants to do per time. It means that there are no significant restrictions keeping the individual from achieving what he intends to achieve at a particular point in time.

Financial freedom can be seen as the leeway that an individual has to be all that he or she desires to be. Also, the person can do all that he or she desires to do per time without worrying about the financial implications.

Also referred to as financial independence, financial freedom refers to the ability to make salient life decisions regardless of how small or big the cost implications are. It also means that when you need to stop working, that is when you reach retirement age, you have money, enough to live well without having to work. (And certainly not totally dependent on family members).

It is undeniably true that money makes the world go round. Let us consider the following situations. You have an emergency that requires quick cash to sort out, or you are planning to be able to live a good life without stress after retirement, or wishing to terminate your present job appointment to develop your skills or invest time do what you have a passion for.

Having plans like these without having to bother about what your bank account is saying is what financial freedom means. In a nutshell, you can plan how you want your life to be and be certain that money will not stand in the way of actualizing such plans.

To some persons, financial freedom is personal, goal specific and subjective. Being financially free means that you have a wide range of options to choose from and you have enough money to make whatever option you choose come to reality.

By the way, it is good to note that financial freedom means different things to different people. Or maybe I should say, to different age classes. We would present that in a different chapter.

To aid the understanding of financial freedom and how it is achieved, we turn to the different types of incomes that exist. The emphasis will be on **active and passive income**.

CHAPTER 2

ACTIVE INCOME

'Active' in this sense means constant, regular or stable. If this term is put together with 'income,' the idea is easily understood. Active income is the remuneration that you receive on a regular basis. It is constant and continuous.

The most basic income in this class is salaries. Salaries are fixed time payments made to you as a result of some services that you have rendered to a firm. They are not the same as the income received from leasing out a house or dividends received from shares.

Some people may not agree that active income can be used as a medium to achieve financial freedom since it is fixed and sometimes not enough to even attend to present needs but that may not be entirely true.

Also, since this book is aimed at acquainting the reader with what financial freedom is, we will consider how active income can be harnessed to attain financial freedom Certain steps may be employed to make active income a stepping stone to financial freedom. I will refer to as **"Strategies for Achieving Financial Freedom from Active Income."**

Here they are:

1. Plan Less Recurrent Spending on Active Income: What does this idea convene to you? First, what are the constituents of recurrent spending?

It is the category of expenses that you make on things which are instantly consumed but which cannot be used for a long period. In short, those non-durables and short-term services, like soft drinks, snacks, movie tickets, hairdo, body cream, etc., all fall into this category.

There are two important features of recurrent spending:

First, they do not constitute things that are indispensable to life, even though they seem to be essential. In fact, life may be better and healthier without them.

Second, they continue to take a large part of income, even though in bits, they seem to be relatively insignificant. This is possibly why their name comes as 're-current': they are short-lived and always need to be redone. (You may pause to run a cursory test on how things in this category work with your expenses and living.) The idea here is not to stop spending recurrently, but to reduce the load of recurrent spending on your active income.

A question may arise on the significance of this plan.

Yes, this plan is very significant. The import of it is that active income is not 'always permanent' income. Certain sudden changes in the environment may stop salaries or other forms of active income that one may be receiving at the moment.

Unforeseen circumstances may arise. Such events can take away the comfort enjoyed from such active income. Hence, the wise and better decision to obtain financial freedom is to plan properly with such active income. It may be unalterably added that financial freedom is not merely independence at the moment only, but independence both at the moment and its guarantee for the farthest future that is attained in the present moment.

2. Plan More Capital Spending on Active Income: As a matter of fact, there does not seem to appear a better way of achieving Plan 1 than by carrying out Plan 2.

This is because it naturally puts the money laying off of less recurrent spending on something more advantageous; it also augments discipline as it expectedly eliminates the possible excuse of lack of profitable things to spend on as a basis of spending on recurrent items.

Did you at this moment just raise an eyebrow as to what capital spending is? Generally, people think capital spending includes buying tangible durables such as houses, landed property, etc. Some others think financial capital such as securities, shares and so on are those things that ideally constitute capital.

Undoubtedly, both views are right. However, there is a newer and better capital good you can use your money on. It is neither tangible nor financial. Education, any good form of education, is worth spending on.

This is the first capital good you should want to consider.

Let us take a quick quiz. Pause a moment and reflect quickly. What are you doing at the moment? Reading? Just going through some random text? I suppose not. I suppose that at this moment, even if you had 'accidentally' found yourself in this act, you have started to orient or reorient yourself in some positive directions owing to the better understanding you have so far got. That is, right now, you are educating yourself.

The intention, of course, is to show that education in this sense is not limited to going to some school, graduating and earning some certificates only.

There is more. It involves you learning through any method you can afford. Spend on workshops, seminars, conferences, etc.

Not only do you learn new things that make you harness your workplace or environment for better income, but also you expand your network and have greater chances of moving up your career. There, you see a capital good worth spending on.

Maybe a lot of emphases has been placed on spending on education; but, it is never meant to be interpreted that you should ignore spending on other important capital goods. The beautiful paradox is that good education teaches you how best to spend on other capital goods.

As simple as these two appear, they are sufficient to help you maximize your active income. If well adopted, this is a step closer to becoming financially independent.

CHAPTER 3

PASSIVE INCOME

What Really is Passive Income?

Again, from the word passive, we may be able to deduce what this kind of income is. Passive refers then income referred to as passive will be payments coming in as a result of the leasing out of a rental property, ownership of a partnership business in which one simply supplies capital.

Basically, the party receiving the passive income is not actively involved in the day to day running of the business enterprise from which such income is received.

Passive income can also be a source where money regularly for doing something once. I mean, check out the life of a blogger. A single blog can generate as many responses as can be, and hours after one blog has been put up, many people get to read and comment, with each response bringing in a specific amount of money.

There are basic features that are associated with passive income. They are:

This kind of income can be taxed but not in the same way as the active income.

It sometimes requires almost no conscious effort on the part of the receiver.

It comes in on a periodic basis

It can be associated with winnings from simply playing a lottery, the earnings on the stock, interest on current or savings account.

It is a lifestyle that promotes the concept of working from home vis a vis being your own boss.

Many believe that having a passive source of income is synonymous with promoting financial freedom. To them, they do not have to rely strictly on the formal job to pay bills or even meet up with emergency demands.

There are different examples of where passive income can be gotten from; this list may not be exhaustive

Rents coming from the ownership of a piece of land that has been leased out to tenants

Interests accruing from a bank account or a pension fund account.

Dividends from the ownership of stocks or other financial security.

Royalties that accrue to the creation/ownership of a music track, a book, a patent for an invention such as software design.

How does one get to earn passive income without stress?

Instead of getting yourself worked up because that job that takes all your day hours and leaves with so stressed at night that you can barely sleep comfortably, why not try out these options for a passive income.

Note that you need to choose a source of passive income that conforms with your personality, your strengths, and flair. Also, you may not need to quit your active job right away, see what "passive job" you can begin with and then work your way through to the top. Alright, let's go:

1. *Consider putting your money into real estate:* You can decide based on the right advice on what property to acquire and in what location to acquire it. Do not be quick to think that real estate only refers to land, of course not! Real estate also includes the natural resources that border the particular land.

You can actually use the space surrounding it to grow crops for additional profits. Who says you cannot get trained personnel to handle the crop planting and cultivation and then you can reap profits from its sale, along with the rents from the building itself. Wow! That sounds fantastic.

2. Buy stocks

Dividends come in as returns on stocks. It means you can acquire some shares today and have it roll over, bringing in dividends for you. You simply need to consult a good stockbroker or an investment banker to find out what company shares you should put your money into. The point is, just a one-time amount can give you a stream of income for a while.

3. Write a book

Come on! It is not that hard!. Just simply pour out your thoughts about a notion that you have a sizeable knowledge about. It could even be about your life experiences. It does not have to be lengthy. Simply, get a good story that a good number of people can relate with, get someone to proofread for you and then publish. You could get a lot of gains from that just one publishing, and peradventure you don't, keep at it, patience is key. Remember the saying "Rome was not built in a day."

4. Become a product marketer

Before you yell at me, it does not have to be a mobile thing. You can create a website, assuming you have a large friend base, get your friends to comment on the product and market the brand through that means. But be sure that such a product has good quality so that people that visit your site another time if they need recommendations on what brand of product to purchase another time.

This simply requires that you liaise with a new or existing company that is trying to gain/regain customer base and loyalty. If you have good marketing, this can be a great spot for you just from the comfort of your home.

5. Engage in online lecturing

This sure sounds like fun for those who love to teach. Yes! And you can make passive income from simply coaching people online on courses that you have a flair for.

You get to choose when and how the lectures would go and trust me if you teach well with proper illustrations and easy language, very busy people who need to take one professional course or two while working may subscribe to your lectures, and then pay for it.

As often as people have need to take such course and get referrals from those who had previously taken them, so often do you get more money from the same lecture notes. Simple.

6. Become a YouTuber

You can make quite some money from making a video and putting it up on YouTube. It does not have to be on an academic course or anything that serious; it could simply be about how you dealt with major experience in your life that you think many people of your age or status may also be struggling with.

It could be on how to prepare a local dish that is not known by many (but appears nice after preparation; this is very key). The catch, however, is to get a large viewer base. But time and social media presence can take care of that.

7. Rent your car out on the weekends for commercial use.

If you have a spare car (for those who do), you can hire one out during the weekends to a reliable commercial driver and then make money from it. There may be some difficulty to this, but having the right person and specifying the area the car should ply amongst others can do the trick. After all, it is better to say, "I tried" than to say, "I was scared of trying."

8. Rent out your cooking utensils

People always have one reason or another to celebrate, and they always have to cook one thing or the other. Why not make use of this opportunity to purchase the big, local cooking pots along with the spoons and rent them out for parties.

It is a cool way of earning a passive income. A onetime purchase can earn you incredible returns especially if you have the right connections to those who have an affinity for celebration.

9. Start out a laundry service business.

This is an evergreen business, simply package your brand well and advertise your services with sample services and then you are good to go. You can simply hire the people who do the washing and ironing and then you simply supervise and give it a unique touch so that it stands out amongst other brands.

10. Enter into a partnership

You may have laudable ideas and do not have the money to execute them, instead of going to debt to finance them, or you may have the idea and the money but need trusted hands to commit them into. Forming a partnership with people who share your dream can help to actualize such dreams faster than if you take on the job yourself. However, take caution as regards who to enter into a partnership with. Do not be scared, there are certainly still good, sincere people out there. I want to believe that you, my dear reader qualify as one.

CHAPTER 4

HOW TO ACHIEVE FINANCIAL FREEDOM.

It is often said that "if you can dream it, then you can achieve it," right? Well, luckily, in achieving financial freedom this is no exception: if you can dream to be financially free, then you really can be. So, why not start dreaming and planning towards it today; Here are practical steps you can take:

Plan your expenses ahead of time

Waiting for the money to come before planning is often a bad choice to make. Why?

Well, simply, because it puts you on the defensive. Why not plan for that income before it comes in? Or plan for that big lottery you are hoping to hit before it finally happens. Have fewer spontaneous spending. Otherwise, spend according to how you have budgeted.

Basically, you need to know this rule of thumb, "no matter how boxed up you are, you still need a plan." Having a planned list of expenses is better than having none at all. This is because it lets you keep check of attending to the things that require urgent or first place attention before others. And many times, for the person who has the view of staying financially free, the first things on his list is to invest in a lucrative venture to get him more money.

So, all we have said so far is that having a budget on what to spend on and how much to spend on each item based on one's item is germane to attaining financial freedom. Be warned that this does not come easily. It requires some level of discipline, self-control, and self-checks in order to make plans and more importantly, stick with them. But dear reader, find solace in these words "nothing good comes easy." The rules are not about to change!

Stay off debt/work towards all debt settlement

Being constantly in debt while hoping to be financially free is a no-no. One sure way of attaining financial freedom is to keep off the habit of borrowing to spend, it is called; living above your means. If you already are in debt, it is proper to work towards repaying it as soon as possible. Having financial freedom means that you need to have your full income to yourself and not just a fragment after the bulk of it has been spent.

Settling off debt will go a long way in setting the foundation for the freedom that you so wish to have. Work at clearing them all, to the tiniest one. (And please! do not go on to acquire some more as soon as that is done.)

This is one good way to go about it. While you should work at settling your debt quickly, do not make the mistake of giving in a huge chunk of your income that you have so little or nothing left for emergencies. That can be disastrous I must say. Again, planning comes in quite handy here, decide on how much you would need for the period till the next paycheck comes in to handle your basic daily needs, coming off a fraction of emergencies. This fraction is not usually the same across the board.

For example, the one who is the firstborn of the family may likely have more emergencies than the last born. The unmarried versus the married, and so on. But the point is, see that you clear all your debt in record time but not at the expense of saving for emergencies.

Make a wise choice of career

This would imply that the job that you should look out for should be one that you enjoy doing and also gives you the opportunity to pursue your goal of financial security. Here is what I mean;

When deciding what job to put in for or what offer to accept, first consider the following:

What is my picture of myself in the future?

Does this job suit my personality?

Does it allow me time to develop myself in order key areas that will eventually improve my work performance?

Does the job come along with employment benefits such as retirement benefits, insurance benefits, retirement saving plan?

What is the size of the salary? Can I say that it would increase with time?

Develop a savings plan

"Save for the rainy day." This is certainly a cliché that is evergreen. There is need to have a savings plan that is adaptable to your goal of financial freedom. After all that debt has been settled, walk up to a savings advisor or qualified bank personnel or a cooperative (whichever suits your itinerary) and commit yourself to a short-term saving plan.

Be sure to assess the progress of your savings from time to time and work at increasing it as your income expands.

INVEST! INVEST!! INVEST!!!

Now that you have accumulated some amount of money in savings, the next wise thing to do is invest. There are tons of investment opportunities lying about everywhere, some investment options are riskier than others, so depending on your level of risk tolerance and the proceeds you intend to get annually as returns, you can decide on what to invest on.

Real estate is one sure area that you can look into to invest your money. Purchasing lands and then leasing them out for ceremonies and events brings juicy returns. All in all. Get in touch with an investment analyst to help and guide you to make that decision.

ACTIVELY KEEP YOUR GOAL OF FINANCIAL FREEDOM

Remember, we started by saying that "if you can dream...". Well, the key to remaining active in your journey towards financial freedom is to keep dreaming.

Keep making active decisions with your goal in mind. Review them periodically and make adjustments where necessary. Just keep your goal in mind – FINANCIAL FREEDOM PATIENCE

A sizeable dose of patience will do you a whole lot of good. You'll see how in a beat. From the time when you start out looking for that dream job, you need to patiently weigh all the options against the list already presented. You'll need to patiently seek the right advice on what to invest your accumulated savings in. You also need patience in watching that investment yield its returns in trickles. And of course! In settling the debt, you need to exercise patience to see it through.

DISCIPLINE

I would like to say that Patience goes along with discipline. The fellow who is determined to attain financial freedom will be disciplined in managing his money well, making plans on what and how to spend while following through with them strictly.

Basically, discipline is to be imbibed in order to arrive at financial freedom.

No obsession, please!

While taking large strides consistently to attain your goal, please, do not get so obsessed with the idea. You know, there is a thin line between determination and obsession. The latter can make you overly sacrifice present happiness for future gains. Even family needs, generous giving and offering assistance to friends in need should not be sacrificed on the altar of trying to secure financial freedom. All in all, be discreet and considerate of the needs of your loved ones while making your plans on how much to save, how much time to devote to self-development and so on. Remember, no man is an island on his own.

What does it mean to be really free?

Financial freedom means many things to many people, and we would look at it going by the different age groups that we have: here we go:

The teenager: to that young girl ages 13 to 19, financial freedom may mean that she now have your own savings, enough to buy her choice lingerie without mummy or daddy deciding the color or size (that can be really gross sometimes!). It also means she has enough money to stack up sanitary towels for as long as can be, without having to run to mummy when the monthlies appear. It basically means that the financial ties to mum and dad are gradually being cut. "I am a big girl now," she wants to say.

The young adult: the young adult life for me beings at say age 20 (there may be other versions, this is simply mine). From ages 20 - 30, the thoughts of one who hopes to be financially free are usually in the line of "I must get my own place." "I can't be under the same roof anymore." "I need to get a good paying job that allows me time to connect and hang out with my friends. To the young adult, therefore, financial freedom is centered on being able to acquire a good job that pays well enough to live a comfortable life.

The "older" adult: from age 30 to 50 (again, this is just my estimations), financial freedom may mean; being able to comfortably fend for your kids, pay their fees, give them the kind of life you have wished for them and still not be looking miserable (you know what I mean, right?). Okay, if you don't, it means that you can still look good and attractive for your spouse, you can still fuel your car and afford your favorite meals at a restaurant. It means you can pay school fees in good time, not after a month or two of expiration.

To the hired employee: financial freedom may have a slightly different meaning to an employee than it may have to a self-employed person. To the former, being able to secure a well-paying job that offers a host of employment benefits and an option of a savings retirement plan. To the self-employed, however, financial freedom may imply having loyal customers who transact and make payments as at when due. He is then able to comfortably plan based on such projections. He can have regular savings that he does not need to revert to until after an elapsed period; he can also expand his business and probably get someone to handle other arms of business while he simply gets the reports and the profits.

To the retired worker: Retirement ages can be very traumatizing, especially for the individual who has no tangible amount of savings stored up somewhere. If such a fellow has to depend on his family or relative (assuming that he has such relations), that definitely does not denote financial freedom.

Financial freedom to a retiree would, therefore, mean that you never have to worry about whether your family sends you weekly or monthly stipends. You can comfortably have your friends come around to hang out with you while you do not have to worry about the cost of hosting them, you can take an online course for simple aesthetic purposes,(this goes to the bookworms, no offense). Or you could even donate a thing or two to charity, all on your own without having to bug anyone about it.

CHAPTER 5

WHAT SHOULD FINANCIAL FREEDOM MEAN TO ME?

Some of us really started out on a rough background, having to fend for ourselves from an early age. You may have had friends, relatives or neighbors who went from being very rich to become very poor. Alas! We may have felt at one point in time in our lives that our parents could have given us a better life if they had planned wisely on how many children to have and/or what sources would they get money from to cater adequately for the children. This, amongst others, may have informed your drive to attain financial freedom and wade off the stress of having to think first of the cost implications before carrying out or making salient life decisions. But hey! I am here to offer some perspective on what financial freedom should mean to you or mean to us.

1. Do not aim at financial freedom to spite others. Instead, do it in order not to be a leech on anyone.

2. Also, aim at financial freedom because it would mean that you are open to tapping into every area where you have your strengths.in other words, seek to be free because it would bring out the very best in you as you search within yourself to bring out the real you.

3. Seek financial freedom to be a model for others to follow. Aim to be successful at

whatever you intend to do to earn a passive income so that others can draw inspiration from what you did and be inspired.

CONCLUSION

Thank you again for downloading this book!

I hope this book was able to help you understand the concept of financial freedom and offer practical ways to achieve financial freedom using both your active and passive income. Remember to imbibe the traits needed to achieve financial freedom as discussed and then watch your dreams come into reality. Cheers!

Finally, if you enjoyed this book, then I would like to ask you for a favor, would please be kind enough to leave a review for this book? It'd be greatly appreciated! Please kindly put in a good word of the knowledge you just acquired.

Thank you and good luck!

www.ingramcontent.com/pod-product-compliance
Lightning Source LLC
Chambersburg PA
CBHW070950180426
43194CB00041B/2034